# Fear of Flying

## *How to Overcome Your Fear of Flying in 10 Easy Steps*

by Christine Hayward

# Table of Contents

Introduction ................................................................... 1

Ch 1: Facts of Flying and De-Bunking Common Myths ........ 7

Ch 2: How to Conquer Your Fear in 10 Easy Steps ............. 13

Conclusion .................................................................... 27

# Introduction

Flying is a great way to get from point A to point B. It is very safe and time-efficient, but there are still many who have flight anxiety or a fear of flying, or aviophobia. Many of these people respond to this fear by not flying at all, which limits them in various ways. Some of these individuals have had flight anxiety for most of their lives, while others have been flying comfortable for a long time, and suddenly develop this condition due to unexpected factors. Sadly, a lot of people who experience flight anxiety resort to pharmaceutical or alcoholic means just to be able to fly.

While most people who are afraid of flying are most fearful of the plane crashing, others actually suffer from claustrophobia, where being "trapped" in a flying "container" feels like too much to handle. It is believed that approximately 1 out of every 6 people are aviophobic, making it one of the most common phobias today. The Anxiety Disorders Association of America characterizes a phobia as an excessive fear of an object or situation, and exposure to such can cause anxious responses including panic attacks. No matter how unreasonable the fear is, people with phobias are often unable to control their fear.

People suffering from this kind of phobia can even exhibit physiological reactions including nausea, rapid breathing, rapid heartbeat, and sweating. However, there are certain steps that can be taken to completely overcome aviophobia. While the fear might currently be a challenge to for those suffering from it, it doesn't need to continue to be.

In this ebook, we will discuss the ten steps it takes to get rid of the fear of flying. But first, let's review (and debunk) some of the things people worry about that causes the fear in the first place.

© Copyright 2014 by LCPublifish LLC - All rights reserved.

This document is geared towards providing reliable information in regards to the topic and issue covered. The publication is sold with the idea that the publisher is not required to render accounting, officially permitted, or otherwise, qualified services. If advice is necessary, legal or professional, a practiced individual in the profession should be ordered.

- From a Declaration of Principles which was accepted and approved equally by a Committee of the American Bar Association and a Committee of Publishers and Associations.

In no way is it legal to reproduce, duplicate, or transmit any part of this document in either electronic means or in printed format. Recording of this publication is strictly prohibited and any storage of this document is not allowed unless with written permission from the publisher. All rights reserved.

The information provided herein is stated to be truthful and consistent, in that any liability, in terms of inattention or otherwise, by any usage or abuse of any policies, processes, or directions contained within is solely and completely the responsibility of the recipient reader. Under no circumstances will any legal responsibility or blame be held against the publisher for any reparation, damages, or monetary loss due to the information herein, either directly or indirectly.

Respective authors own all copyrights not held by the publisher.

The information herein is offered for informational purposes solely, and is universal as so. The presentation of the information is without contract or any type of guarantee assurance.

The trademarks that are used are without any consent, and the publication of the trademark is without permission or backing by the trademark owner. All trademarks and brands within this book are for clarifying purposes only and are the owned by the owners themselves, not affiliated with this document.

# Chapter 1: Facts of Flying and De-Bunking Common Myths

There are a lot of things that trigger people to have flight anxiety. Aviophobia is not something that many people naturally have. Rather, it's commonly when people often hear scary yet seemingly sensible information from others that makes them question if flying is safe. The truth of the matter is, much of the information is often false and does not have a lot of foundation.

Here are a few of the myths that cause people to become afraid of going up in the sky.

**Myth #1: The plane can "shut-down" while in flight**

When people look at planes, they often wonder, "What if the plane, all of a sudden, shut down while in flight?" This is nearly impossible today in commercial airplanes because they have many backup power sources. Flight systems for commercial planes often have at least one, and up to four, backups which vary according to the type of aircraft. Most airliners today have multiple engines and each of these engines has their own generator, meaning it is next to impossible for an airplane to simply drop out of the sky due to a total system failure. Even pilots have backups, remember?

## Myth #2: The airplane's door might open suddenly

Thanks to Hollywood and a string of "Final Destination" scenes, a lot of us think we have a good idea of what can happen if a door of an aircraft opens mid-flight. Flying at around 30,000+ feet high, the cabin of any airplane is pressurized to simulate the atmospheric pressure when you are on land. The pressure outside is not the same, so if a hole opens up, you will get sucked out if your seatbelt is not secured, as seen in countless movies that feature an airplane crash scene. However, remember that these scenes never feature a door actually opening. The crashes are all caused by some kind of accident like a bullet hitting a window and smashing the glass. The fact of the matter is, the door of an aircraft is impossible to open while in flight. The higher pressure inside the airplane basically pushes against the door, effectively wedging it in position. You could not open the door, even if you wanted to. It would take tons of pressure to open an aircraft door at a 35,000 foot elevation. This is one of the reasons why you will not see skydiving planes venture to the height that commercial airlines are able to. An aircraft is designed to exploit the laws of physics to improve safety, and this is an example of just that.

## Myth #3: The aircraft might suddenly lose lift and drop out of the sky

Thankfully, again, the laws of physics make this impossible. There are many elements that shift things in our favor when it comes to flying. The first is the principle of lift. Lift is what keeps the aircraft flying, while the engine is what propels it forward. The reason larger planes have more engines is to be able to propel forward fast enough to achieve the lift needed to fly. Throughout the flight, the plane becomes lighter and thus has more lift. Even if all of the engines of a commercial airliner fail, there is always the 3:1 rule, meaning that for every altitude drop in 1,000 feet, the plane will have traveled 3 miles forward. So at 39,000 feet (the flight altitude of most commercial airliners), the plane will have traveled more than 115 miles forward. If no land is in sight, the aircraft is designed to handle a water landing and float. Who can forget the January 2009 Hudson landing by Captain Chesley Sullenberger?

**Myth #4: A single bird can bring down a plane**

While bird strikes are a threat for some single-engine planes, they are hardly an issue for an aircraft with multiple engines. A common airliner has four widely spaced engines which makes it impossible for all of the engines to experience a mid-air bird strike and malfunction. In addition, airplane engines have been continually improved so that they can continue to function even after a direct hit. An example of the improvements is the metal makeup of the fan blades. A commercial aircraft can stay in flight, even with a single engine, so don't worry about a bird bringing down the bird that you are in.

There are a lot more things that people wonder about planes, leading them to doubt airplane dependability. However, the airplane has been around for over a century, and is continually being improved for safety and efficiency, so you don't have a lot to worry about. Even older aircrafts still in operation are being continually updated to allow the accommodation of more sensors and upgraded navigation and safety systems.

Okay, so let's admit: a phobia is a phobia, precisely because it is irrational and sometimes even illogical. Even after debunking these myths, I don't expect that you're magically cured of your phobia quite yet. However, that does not mean that there is absolutely nothing you can do about it, so let's keep going.

# Chapter 2: How to Conquer Your Fear in 10 Easy Steps

For people with flight anxiety or a fear of flying, the idea of flying itself can cause them to altogether freak out, and even experience panic attacks. Those with flight anxiety are willing to go through a lot of trouble, preferring to travel for hours by land to avoid getting on a plane even though it dramatically cuts down on travel time. But remember, statistically, flying is a lot safer than driving. The chances of you dying in a plane crash are 1 in 10 million, compared to a 1 in 5000 chance of a car crash death.

Many have this fear because they are not the one in control of the plane, unlike when they are driving. You also have to remember that air traffic is a lot lighter than vehicular traffic on the road, and even though you are in control of your vehicle when driving, you are not in control of how other drivers behave. Most road accident victims and casualties are exactly that, victims. They died because of someone else. Yet, for some reason, plane crashes get more notoriety and thus a greater fear factor. Even so, there are things that we can do get over the fear and actually enjoy the experience of flying. Think of it this way: Some people even enjoy jumping out of airplanes… so it shouldn't be that hard to stay in one, right?

## Step 1: Identify the Specifics of Your Fear

The first step of getting over your fear is to know the source of it, and give it a name. Just like any fight, you need to know who your enemy is first. Flight anxiety is often triggered by other things including turbulence that the aircraft experiences in takeoffs and landings. This is perfectly normal, since the air is providing lift but is not as smooth as we think. All aircrafts experience turbulence in almost all of their flights. Pilots are trained to handle things a lot worse than turbulence.

Germophobic tendencies can also be triggered, since you are going to be in a confined space that you share with a lot of people. Even in first class, you still share the same air with everybody else because you are inside an enclosed and pressurized area.

Claustrophobia is also a concern when boarding an airplane, which in turn causes a lot of anxiety since you are thousands of feet in the air in a flying tube. A lot like being in an elevator, an airplane has a tendency of making one feel trapped, since essentially, you are.

A large majority of people who are afraid of flying, are actually mostly fearful of being overwhelmed with anxiety on the flight, although they are not afraid of the concept of flying, itself.

By definition, a phobia is irrational to begin with, but identifying the cause makes it easier to address it. As with any problem, the first step is to know what you are dealing with. So before moving on, force yourself to identify specifically which specific aspect(s) of flying that's the source of your fear.

**Step 2: Know What to Expect**

Half the battle with any fear is proper preparation so that nothing catches you off guard. For example, knowing – and reminding yourself – to expect loud noise and turbulence will prevent you from becoming anxious because of these occurrences when you experience them in flight. So remember, the airplane is a large craft with very large engines, so they will make a lot of noise. And when the plane takes off, it will inevitably run into turbulence, which is also normal. For people who are used to smooth rides, turbulence can be quite traumatic since they believe that the airplane is floating on air. It is not floating on thin air; the plane needs a lot of air to pass under the wings to keep you up in the sky and this is what creates the turbulence. If you look at it this way, turbulence is nothing more than a small bump in the road when you're driving. You would not stop driving just because you've hit a rough patch on a road. Certain noises, like the seat belt bell, can also trigger anxiety since a lot of people think that if the seat belt light is on, then things might be heading south, but expecting these things and knowing that they are perfectly normal will be helpful in lessening the fear of being in a plane.

Also, many first-time flyers are quite anxious when the plane that they are in is going through bad weather. They think that the plane will simply shut down and drop out of the sky if it gets hit by lightning. Believe it or not, pilots have a lot of weather specific sensors that tell them what the weather is like ahead. If the situation is more than they and the plane can handle, they have ample time to go around it. Lightning is also not enough to bring a plane down, because the plane is made of materials that are great conductors. But again, preparing yourself for flying in bad weather – with the knowledge that the pilots are aware of the weather conditions in advance and that the plane won't encounter any weather beyond what is considered safe according to the industry safety regulations – will prevent you from becoming overly stressed out by it in the event that you actually experience it.

## Step 3: Remember that Airplanes Are Designed to Survive Turbulence

Airplanes have been developed to not resist but cut through air, and this causes perfectly normal bumps and shaking. Although the shaking can remind us of earthquakes, in this case, turbulence is not that bad. Pilots are also trained to fly with minimal concern of turbulence. Remember that pilots are human beings too, and they are at the front of the plane. They are trained to recognize when conditions are too much for the plane to handle, and thus, they will not enter a cloud formation that could cause a lot of problems for the plane. The point is, turbulence is normal, and there is no reason to associate it with an earthquake or an air crash. Just like your automaker sent your car through a lot of testing, long before it was available for sale, all aircrafts have been designed to survive the worse kind of turbulence. Every plane experiences turbulence, so this is not a symptom of something bad every time it happens.

**Step 4: Think of Your Destination**

Obviously, you are going somewhere, which is why you are boarding a plane. A great way to address flight anxiety is to think of your destination or, better yet, look at a photo. This takes your mind off the fear and allows you to focus on something positive. It can be an actual printed picture or a downloaded one in your phone. "Find your happy place," as others might say. It can be your bedroom or a beach; go there by closing your eyes and imagine yourself relaxing. The idea is that you need to focus your mind on something positive and not the fear. This relaxes you and makes flying a more enjoyable affair. All physical reactions start in the mind. If your mind is not focused on the fear and is busy thinking of something positive, it will not have time to worry about things that you do not need to be worrying about in the first place. Coming on the plane with a proper mindset is your first protection against anxiety. As I mentioned earlier, you have to look at this as a fight. And if you come in to a fight thinking that you will lose, then that is exactly what will happen. Alternatively, concentrating on your destination is the same as thinking that you have won the fight, and thereby this is an important step in totally overcoming flight anxiety.

## Step 5: Skip the Cup of Coffee

Taking in caffeine before a flight is not a good idea, since it has the potential to increase your sensitivities to, and awareness of, things that you normally wouldn't even notice or care about. You are often on edge and more alert when you consume caffeine, which makes normal things seem more alarming. But also, skip the pre-flight drink. Any alcohol intake at all can make your body react negatively when you are airborne, and can bring about some serious dehydration and jetlag. Water or a light pre-flight snack sounds a lot better and can help you sleep like a baby for the whole flight.

## Step 6: Watch a Movie or Read a Book

Quite simply, distraction is the golden key for any savvy traveler, and especially one with a fear of flying. If you are someone who likes reading books or magazines, make sure that you bring one (or several) on your flight, and start reading well before the plane is taxiing. Reading a book can allow your imagination to take charge, keeping your mind off the fear entirely. Watching a movie or watching the in-flight TV programming options is also a great way to distract yourself. Watching a movie will not only take your mind away from the flight, but it can keep you from hearing the mechanical noises that can trigger the anxiety. Watching a TV series also relaxes you, in a way, because your body and mind reacts as it would normally do at home, making you feel much more within your own "comfort zone."

## Step 7: Be Friendly and Honest

Being friendly with the flight attendants can be quite useful and letting them in on your phobia can go a long way. When they know you're not at ease flying, they'll be sure to make you more a lot more comfortable and keep an eye out for signs of anxiety. Sure, that is their job, but if the flight attendants understand that you are not the usual flyer, they know that they will have to make you feel more comfortable than the other passengers, and they're trained to do so. You're not doing this to intentionally make yourself special; a genuine phobia does require a bit more care and attention. Who knows, you might even get to meet the pilot so that he or she can let you know how safe it is. Flight attendants are naturally caring and helpful, not to mention well-trained in spotting signs of anxiety; in case you do start feeling uneasy, don't think twice before letting them know.

## Step 8: Don't Miss the Safety Briefing

Since most phobias are due to a fear of dying, paying attention to the safety briefing before the plane takes off is a great idea. Feeling confident that you know exactly what to do in emergencies will put your mind at ease, as will knowing that the crew of the plane also knows what to do in the worst-case scenario. Furthermore, you'll find it quite assuring that you have a great chance of surviving due to the safety measures put in place, and yet an even larger chance of nothing happening at all.

Airplanes are also regularly maintained in terms of their safety features, which means that you are on a craft that has passed hundreds of safety checks. If you really want to feel safe, book a seat that is more or less at the back of the plane, because statistically, the back is the best place to be in a worst-case scenario.

## Step 9: Relaxation Breathing

Take in deep breaths through the nose and exhale from the mouth. This is important because oxygen can help you relax and relieve anxiety. Start by trying to hold your breath, then breathe in deep and exhale slowly. This allows you to relax and it prevents hyperventilation. To keep your airways open, be sure that you keep your back straight and maintain good posture. It also helps to get a seat that is not next to the window, since the sight of the ground getting farther and farther away could cause your heart to beat faster. Pretend like you are just in a bus, since an airplane is a lot like a bus anyway. This way, you can pretend that the turbulence is just bumps on the road.

## Step 10: Have a Fail-Safe Option Handy

Normally, medication is not the best way to overcome anxiety, but it does not hurt to have some with you just in case. Actually having it with you and knowing that you "could" take it if you wanted to is often times enough to help you feel more relaxed and "in control", such that you don't even need to take it. You'll need to get a prescription from your doctor for anxiety reducing pills, such as Valium or Xanax. But remember, if you do end up taking something, you may experience other negative side effects, for example feeling exhausted (even after the plane lands), or even developing a dependency or addiction. Talk to your doctor to learn more about the potential side effects. But keep in mind, as mentioned, the actual purpose for having the pills with you isn't to take them. It's just to give you the sense of control that goes with having them available and deciding on your own that you don't need them. A mind trick.

# Conclusion

Flight anxiety is more common than a lot of people think, especially after 9/11 and other heavily reported airplane tragedies. However, this does not mean that we're trapped and have to feel scared when we are in a plane, or worse, opting to drive for hours when we can travel by air for only one hour. At the end of the day, you are the one who can overcome your own flight anxiety. These ten steps can either be your saving grace or they may just be the first of many things that you will try in order to enjoy a flight, instead of being scared. In any case, you'll need to make a concerted effort to overcome your fear so that you can enjoy traveling by air.

Flying can be a very pleasurable experience as long as you can keep your anxiety level in check or, better yet, get rid of it as a whole. It all starts in the mind. Just like fighting, you need to know what enemy you are actually facing, know what you will experience, and remember that the plane is designed to endure a lot, even multiple lightning strikes.

Finally, remind yourself of the benefits and facts of flying: that it's not only faster than driving for long distances, but it is also a lot safer. The only reason that air crashes are as reported and as tragic as they are, is because they carry hundreds of people at a time. Yet, remember that thousands of airplanes take off and land every single day without any problems. We live in a world where statistics makes a lot more sense than superstitious beliefs, which is an advantage since you are a lot safer flying than driving. Planes are safe and are continually being improved, so you can expect to have even fewer problems associated with flying in the future than there are now… and there really aren't many now to begin with.

Finally, I'd like to thank you for purchasing this book! If you found it helpful, I'd greatly appreciate it if you'd take a moment to leave a review on Amazon. Thank you!

Printed in Great Britain
by Amazon